SUMMER ROSE TO THE OCCASION

SUMMER ROSE TO THE OCCASION

Lisa Coppage

Summer Rose to the Occasion

Published by Gatekeeper Press

7853 Gunn Hwy., Suite 209
Tampa, FL 33626

www.GatekeeperPress.com

ISBN (hardcover): 9781662951336

ISBN (paperback): 9781662951343

eISBN: 9781662951350

This book is dedicated to my amazing daughter and awesome son-in-law and their daughters. Also, to all who have experienced unbearable pain and loss, may this book bring you comfort and hope to know that your light will shine bright again.

TABLE OF CONTENTS

PREFACE

This book was inspired by Summer Rose "Bum-Bum," my first and eldest granddaughter, whose mission was to labor through the earth with us long enough to give the family the greatest message of all, a message that changed our lives forever. This is a true story inspired by an infant who shared her experience with her grandmother's spirit as she witnessed how gently the message was delivered to her parent's heart to cherish a keepsake for her beloved siblings and family forever.

CHAPTER 1

Summer Rose to the Occasion

How could someone so little have such an enormous impact on so many? As she contoured her little body so quietly and gently jelled to her mother's soul, she spoke the words inner-spiritedly to us and whispered privately in each one's ear:

I cannot stay because Heaven is waiting for my return. Mommy, you were chosen and handpicked for me. As God was preparing for my arrival, I heard your strong voice pulsating from your heartbeat to mine. You told me that you would never forget me and that you would love me forever. Mommy, you hummed tunes and gently caressed your hands around your stomach which gave me the comfort of knowing that you are going to be a caring mommy and would never erase me from your thoughts.

Although my time on this earth seemed short, Daddy, I was here before you were formed in grandma's belly. Mommy, I was already in your future before you knew what it meant. This was aligned for me to come and deliver the message. What message do you ask? It was to take nothing for granted, forgive yourself and each other daily, appreciate what you have, and enjoy family and friends now. Avoid putting off things for today instead of tomorrow because each day is a gift from God. Never go to sleep angry; instead talk about it, whatever it is. Tell your family and friends that you love them, don't be afraid to say you made a mistake, apologize or forgive them, show compassion and empathy for others, don't be too prideful to ask for help, have faith to believe, and remember what you send out into the atmosphere will return to you. Love yourself, forgive yourself, leave your past back there, and come up here to your full potential and purpose in life.

Didn't you see that I lived through you both? Your face, eyes, and nose are mine. Your laughter is being heard, and I can still feel your touches. Can you feel mine? When you hear the rain, I'm talking. When you smell the flowers, it's me kissing your nose. I love how you take care of Mommy and my sisters. I'll enjoy watching you cut the grass. I'm the butterflies and ladybugs and, at times, the bees chasing after you. I'm here, Daddy when you're wondering how it would have been. I'm right here when you look into Mommy's eyes. I'm looking back at you. My sisters know me, and when you're ready, let them know I love them very much and will always be with them. There'll be times you may notice them laughing or smiling or even looking far off into space. No need to worry they're being entertained by angels, and I just may be in the midst. There is no reason to wonder why things happened the way that they did. It does not take away from the love that I gave and still give. My love produced love, and my siblings will respect the power of love.

I know that my sudden departure left a bitter taste in all your mouths, but it also built strength in all of you that you did not know you possessed. If you look at it with your eyes, it seems like a loss, but when you look through it with your heart, you'll find out that it is such a huge gain because the pain grew you to a new level of understanding. If you can imagine a lullaby to share with my siblings, imagine that I returned to the garden, and my ancestors greeted me with hugs and kisses. Welcoming me back from my assignment, they explained to me how the Creator was pleased and that He knew you and Daddy before you were in your mommies' bellies. It is always extra special telling stories about you guys and learning some of the reasons why things happened. I'm told that sometimes we will never know.

This garden is filled with harmony and peace, everyone is treated respectfully and nicely, we don't take anything for granted, and nothing forbidden can enter into this place. It's not like your world where people are unforgiving, mean, cruel, refuse to love, and seem to enjoy

Daddy, your world was scary. My world is a peaceful garden filled with lots of lovely people and serene sounds with lots of friendly animals. In this peaceful garden, there are other babies like me, and we play well together, laugh, crawl, walk, run, and wobble all around just like I did in Mommy's belly. Everything is provided for us and plentiful—fruits, vegetables, songs. We take great pleasure surrounding ourselves with our Creator and tribes. There are no fears, tears, pain, hurt, or shame. It is simply sweet, wonderful, and the best part of it all. I am happy here, and I am being taken care of too.

So, when you tell my siblings about me or share my story with the world, remember that I came to deliver a message of healing. It was my assignment, and it had to be carried out by me. You and Daddy cared, nourished, and provided physically, but it was a greater cause spiritually. I had to complete the assignment. Everyone has an assignment, even babies like me, and you must be ready when it is time to deliver.

Please don't be sad, because in my world there isn't sadness. It's light and full of life. Sometimes, I sit around and listen to the Creator of the universe teach us lessons and show us what is going on in your world and what will come out of it. At times, the Creator arranged for the ancestors to also teach us lessons about dreams and visions. Sometimes, we visit friends and loved ones in their dreams. I especially enjoy this assignment because it brings comfort to so many, and sometimes, the Creator will go the extra mile to give you what we call an "impression." That's when you might hear your loved one's voice, feel a soft hand on your shoulder or a ladybug or butterfly, or even some other animal might find you nearby. You might smell a familiar scent, hear a favorite song, or even sometimes angels might entertain you by playing "the missing game." It's like when you lay something down and you go back to get it and it is not there, but then you'll find it in a familiar place that may remind you of a loved one. Maybe you'll see someone who looks like one of your loved ones. A baby might smile at you or walk up to you and reach for your finger. This may bring memories and some tears but not to be sad but comforted. Remember my message was to bring healing, not only to our family but to others. All I'm trying to say is, don't get so busy with life that you miss the little things that greatly matter.

Back to my garden, I have been told that many years ago, this place was prepared for all of us. However, when men became prideful and greedy and stole and lied to us, this behavior caused division, and those people were cut off from our tribe. The faithful ones were given keys and instructions to the garden and charged to complete assignments.

I know that I was loved and am still loved. I know I'll never be forgotten. I know it may be difficult to mention me from time to time, but please remember that I came to bring healing to our family and others. Although it was a short visit, I still rose to the occasion. It was you and Daddy's assignment to put the pieces together, and you both did it in a unified and graceful way. You supported and comforted each other. You showed others what strength looked like even when it hurt. What a courageous way to be!

I am honored to have shared a loving and memorable inner experience with you both. Upon my departure, there were new levels of awareness, knowledge, understanding, tenderness, and happiness that evolved into an unspeakable joy that formed an uninterrupted and unbreakable bond that made it so easy to manifest into a love that neither one of you thought could grow even deeper. During this revelation, my sister was in the making and was well-informed about how to handle the things of your universe.

You both are correct when you say she's been here before. She has visited from time to time, and you and Daddy were handpicked for her parents. I am proud of my family, and although I cannot be there naturally, I am always there in spirit because I am spirit!

CHAPTER 2

Reign Brings Life

About my siblings... Laila is a loving little girl, and she is going to do great things in your world. She is a kind soul and will learn how to tell the difference between who is good and who is evil. She will learn to hone her gifts because there are many. She is strong and already knows what she likes and does not like. So by now, you both should have realized that it is in your DNA. Laila will enjoy drawing and working with her hands. This is one of her gifts that will make room for many achievements. She is the one who will enjoy learning lots of things outdoors. Daddy, take advantage of this. You will soon see how this will come in handy for you.

Laila and Zöe are going to enjoy cooking and learning family recipes.

The holidays are going to be the best because they aren't going to be like the traditional holidays but more like unique experiences filled with conversation, dancing, familiar and unfamiliar smells in the kitchen, various sounds, and music, which is something we could not escape.

Laila is going to protect little Zöe, no doubt about it. I am watching over them, but Laila is going to "pow-wow" anyone who may appear to be a threat to Zöe. Oh please! Make no mistake, they are kind little girls, but they are going to be tough and unafraid to stand up for each other, and rightfully so, especially in your world.

Again, when you tell them about me, try not to cry but smile and laugh because my spirit will always be there. When you look at my siblings, you must see me. As for the latest addition to my family, embrace all that you will learn about them. They have pieces of yours and Daddy's personalities. So, you can only imagine how I would have been.

Zöe is also known as "ZoZo." She loves

music time, the soft tunes with the slow beat ever so gentle. Zöe is still getting used to her big sister's sounds and sudden moves, but don't worry. They are going to be tight as the fireflies in the night.

She is more demanding than her big sister because she knows what she wants already! Daddy and Mommy, I must admit that they have a mixture of your personalities and gestures. Our Zöe is a force, and everyone she crosses paths with is going to know it. She is going to love music and dance too. She won't mind making people laugh. She is very strong-willed, and when her mind is made up, there is no negotiation. It will be what it will be. Although she is kind, her toughness comes with the help of her big sister Laila. Yep! Big Sister is preparing her already. Zöe is a great student, and Laila is an amazing teacher. But the tables will reverse, and Zöe will become the teacher and Laila the student. They are going to enjoy the family night. Make it special because the girls are going to love the extra attention—that is, until they don't.

Daddy, do you know your girls love to hear your voice radiate throughout the house? Your strong hands swing Laila around. Although, I'm not too sure if Laila is going to enjoy that rushed and woozy feeling; it may have to grow on her. Zöe won't mind getting all of it at once. I love to see the sparkle in Mommy's eyes when she watches you play with my sisters. She loves to hear them laugh and coo. I find myself watching and laughing along with her. Boy! My family is so funny, and your house is a home of love. It gives me so much joy to know that you give them something that neither of you has ever had: a very happy home. Thank you both.

As you begin to learn more about my sisters, don't forget to tell them things about the both of you. Let them hear you say what you love, like, dislike, favorite colors, sports, candy, drinks, foods, and so on.

They are not too young to know or understand because this is how they will learn what love is like in our home. Let them feel your soft touch, see you kiss

Mommy, give them a hug, sit them in your lap, and talk to them about feelings and the importance of having a family to take care of. Enjoy story time. It makes them feel calm and cuddly when they are snuggled in the creases of your arms. They're growing up just like the big girls I knew they would be. So, neither one of you should worry about how they are going to do in this great big world because, with your love and guidance, they will be just fine. After all, both families come from strong tribes filled with energy, wisdom, and strength. There's more to come, and there will always be more to learn.

CHAPTER 3

Yah-Yah

The village must prepare wisely. Active and responsible grandparents are the true village keepers. What are "keepers?" "Keepers," for me, means taking care of yourself, self-caring tools, staying in compliance with your medications and doctor's care, eating well, being aware of your health needs, designating accountable partners or friends and expecting the same from them. This may seem unnecessary now, but when the unexpected shows up in your life, you may not have the time or energy to plan. So, prepare yourself. If you discover that these kinds of people do not exist in your life, then have a mature conversation with the people you are helping. How do you remain prepared and kept? By being unafraid to ask for help, holding yourself accountable, understanding that your feelings matter too, and being mindful to take breaks. For years, our grandparents and ancestors have paved the way for us. Take the time to cultivate and educate your village and hold them responsible for completing their assignments. Grandparents do not have to do it alone. It takes a village to get the job done effectively and promptly.

As I cradled her little body in my hand, what seemed to have been a matter of moments felt like days because, for me, her spirit was alive. I gazed at her precious face, praying that her eyes would open and she would come back to us. My heartbeat sounded so loud. It felt like it was beating outside my chest, and my right arm began to pulsate. I thought it was Summer's heartbeat, but I was wrong. Listening to the moans and then the silence at the same time convinced me to believe that the pain was real, and the void was present.

Summer's spirit was also real. It stirred mine, and I felt a connection. I remembered comforting my daughter as

much as I could and asking the Father to strengthen my son's spirit. I couldn't stop thinking about how my daughter and son must have felt. I knew that they would find the strength to carry on, but I did not know how much time it would take.

As I locked my eyes back on my precious granddaughter's face, an unusual thing happened. A child's voice began to speak to me. Now, I know how strange this may sound, and I was aware and accepted that she was deceased. However, it happened, and I had to embrace the moment to see what it was all about. I have decided to share this experience with the world because I truly believe that there is life after death.

Writing this book took me on an emotional somersault. Nonetheless, I was compelled to complete my assignment in support of other parents, siblings, family members, caretakers, and especially grandparents who may have experienced a similar loss but do not have the words for it. I am aware that grief can play tricks on a person's mind, but there was this calmness and stillness that embodied the entire room.

What I experienced is, in fact, real and necessary to share.

I was left alone in the room with my granddaughter, and after kissing her forehead, I recall hearing a child's soft voice. It was like "Bum-Bum" was telling me a story about why she came and had to leave. I know that she and I were the only ones in the room adjacent to my daughter's room, and no, I did not think

I was losing my mind because I am familiar with spiritual encounters. As I stood rocking her side to side, I listened to the voice that sounded like a little child, and it was my granddaughter who was one day old telling me a story that had never been told. During the uninterrupted time, it was pure, it was happening, and I was present. You may think this is beyond belief, but for me, it was a supernatural miracle.

Perhaps, some like me will believe what I am saying because you too know that spirits don't die, and energy is real. For the unbelievers, you may think this is far-fetched. My assignment does not require me to try to convince you. It requires me to get my message out, and what you do or don't do with it is totally up to you.

I held Summer long enough to receive what she had to say. Being a grandmother, we learn to take it all in, bear the pain of others, and remain strong enough to learn the lesson. I can't tell you how long I held my granddaughter or what was happening outside of that room, but what I can say is that it felt like it had been days. I remembered the nurse stood beside me, and when I no longer heard Summer's voice, I carefully handed her over to the nurse and rushed into the room with my daughter. I held my daughter tight, kissed her face, and told her that we were going to get through this together. I did not share my experience with either of them because my body was exhausted and numb. I had to remain present and available for my daughter and son for the days to come because it was going to be rough, but with all our strengths and leaning on the support of each other, we will get through it.

What a special way to keep our legacy growing. Summer is alive in our hearts because we refuse to forget about her. It is essential to share every emotion we experienced with her in the short time we had. It was a traumatic experience that brought pain, anger, sorrow, joy, love, forgiveness, and growth to our family. I hope that you have gathered the comfort, support, and encouragement you need as you continue to heal from your loss on your journey. I hope you can begin to see just as I did with my granddaughter that someone so small could be used by the Creator to leave behind such an enormous impact on the world.

What a force she is because her spirit lives. Summer Rose left her imprint in the center of our hearts. A part of me wanted to keep her message sealed inside my heart, but that would be selfish. It would have defeated Father's purpose for her life. I realized that the message was not just for my family but for yours too. The Creator orchestrated every step of her little feet that touched this world—"Bum-Bum," who was and will always be loved by many.

This experience inspired me to share her journey in such an impactful way with all of you especially, to bring comfort to the grieving parents, siblings, grandmothers, and other important family members and to leave your stories as a keepsake for all the awesome big brothers or sisters who were not allowed to meet their little sister or brother. May God's perfect peace and healing be with you.

Chapter 4

The Cultivated Tribe

For as long as I can remember, I have always been surrounded by the grands and the greats, either my grandmothers or grandmothers of others, great aunts or great uncles, and so on. However the cookie crumbled, it was always a tribe. My tribe were strong family members who held the responsibility to support each other during a loss or difficult times involving several key aspects.

These were wise women and men who cultivated the traumas in my family. The tribe understood the importance of emotional support that provided comfort, understanding, and a listening ear to those who were grieving or struggling. This kind of support helps alleviate feelings of isolation or loneliness.

The cultivated tribe has a history of lessons learned and what worked. This type of tribe knew what needed to be done before it became a task. They approached it as practical assistance. They offered help with daily tasks and responsibilities that may become overwhelming during difficult times. This sometimes included cooking meals without being asked, taking care of children, managing household chores, and being wise enough to feel the pain without one word being said. These tribes enjoy sharing their wisdom, for it's the elders and experienced family members who share their knowledge and coping strategies, providing guidance, perceptions, and acceptance based on their past experiences.

The cultivated tribe has a strengthening bond that upholds their support for their family. They realize that even the strong cry sometimes, and in their weakest times, there aren't any weakest links because the family strengthens its bonds, fostering a sense of unity and collective resilience.

They have been taught to encourage and motivate each other to stay hopeful and persevere through tough times and losses, reinforcing the belief that challenges can be overcome together. We understand that engaging in our beliefs and support systems is based on God's truth, and a family that stands strong together prays and fights together. We know the power of encouragement provides a sense of stability and continuity, helping family members feel connected to their roots and cultural heritage.

With all said, a tribe of strong family members could be that one individual who ensures that no one faces adversity alone, creating a supportive and nurturing environment that helps everyone navigate through life's challenges, even if that means sharing story time in her granddaughter's company.

9 781662 951343